Yellow

Penguin Poetry
NYC

Follow us on Instagram
@PenguinPoetryNYC

We bring each other up, not pull each other down. We are a community. We are each unique in our voices. And we aren't afraid to use them.

This is our time to rise.

Foreword

When I need inspiration, I think of you. Yes, you. I think of the good, the bad, the ugly, the beautiful, the happy, the sad, and everything in between. I think about what you've experienced — what you've endured, lost, gained, and lost again. I think about your triumphs, your failures. But mostly, I think about your determination. How you didn't give up, no matter how much you wanted to.

And you're still here. Still fighting. Still going. That gives me inspiration. That is why I'm here. That's why you're here. We bring each other up, not pull each other down. We are a community. We are each unique in our voices. And we aren't afraid to use them.

This is our time to rise.

- Sarah Doughty

Song of Eve

I woke to you, naked and familiar,
something under my skin
and deep in my chest
calling as if it belonged to you.
It didn't feel right.
You made sure I knew that
the pain in your side was
caused by me,
that I took something
that belonged to you;
You'd wanted a companion
but not the sacrifice.
I was always under your thumb;
Under God's very command
but He never spoke to me,
only you with your small
idea of paradise and the
fear of knowing what is beyond.
That silver tongued serpent,
the devil's own,
saw your weakness
and knew that a woman's strength
is her mind, not her womb.
He whispered in my ear
honied words of freedom
and so I ate,
intent on escaping you
and your disappointing

lack of imagination.
From that moment on,
I belonged only to myself.

- Kris Duncan

The Storm

Sometimes
I am the storm.

And sometimes,
I am the kite
Trapped in a storm,
Getting shredded by it.

- Debjyoti Ghosh

Gifted Regret

My love was a gift.
You ripped off the ribbon,
Tore through the wrapping,
Took one look,
Handed it back to me and said,
"I already have one of these."

- Wade Staark

Illusion of Love

My mind's figmental
Dreaming you into my life
Perverse imagination

Conjured through my dreams
Falling for a fictitious you
Unendurable

Consumed with desire
Running around in circle
Reasoning it out

I thought it was love
But you are just another
Idea in my head

Trying to seek help
Sanity slipping away
Quashing you from my mind

Daily injections
Alternate shock therapies
Doesn't seem to work

Haloperidol
Keeping me in custody
You're still in my dream

Trying hard to claw
Your reverie in my skin
Slashing 'til it bleeds

A padded white room
Restrained by the straightjacket
Thinking about you

Illusion of love
I really thought it is love
I thought it was love

- Britt H

Addict

Love has
beat the
living shit
out of me
enough times
to count;
I'm a fucking
addict
who loves
the taste
of his
own blood.

- Myke Duarte Carlos

Permission

You do not have to
hide the rattle in your bones
under fake smiles.

Take the pin out of the grenade
you have under your ribcage.
Let love explode and
paint your walls red.
The grey doesn't look
calm anymore.

You do not have to
turn down the volume
of your emotions.
Give your brain
the permission to sing
a happy song.

I know you think
dark is the colour for you.

But my love,
have you seen yourself lately?
Light looks magnificent on you.

-Swati Barik

Mon Adieu

I felt unclothed under one of
Your many gazes.
The others – your shy, intoxicated smile,
As if you couldn't believe your good fortune.
I wish I could store it and
Age it like fine wine.

How did you feel under a sky
As blue as curiosity?
You held me like fruit you'd like to bruise.
This passion shared under
Whistling crimson sails.
My sensitive poet, a schoolboy in blue jeans.

I shot for the moon, but wound up in the sea.
Fortunately, I'm a good swimmer.
Threw me for a curve.
Sometimes I still find myself orbiting around.

I love what your roots grasp.
You're diamond-hard,
Shadowed only by your brilliance,
A star waiting to go nova.

This pseudo love affair
Celebrated with high fives and cartwheels.
A fairytale in July.
The things that are revealed through yawns

And when we're in our cups.
You asked for my honesty.
I said your name,
But never mind.
I only footnoted it with God's.

This magic amidst the mystery,
I thought it was ripening to full maturity.
I'd watch you struggle
With something within yourself
As I stroked your damp skin.

I didn't realize your perspective was askew.
You'll pussy foot around the issues,
And I'll remain ambiguous.
Confessions will give way to
Frightful silences.

Imperfection is not your ideal.
I'll keep your image safe
Behind crystal-blue glass.

It's all so simple,
So don't worry.

I'm not Ophelia.

- Erin Suurkoivu

Subway Scars

Train rides in my brain
Static windows
We all smell the same,
There's a story
In an old woman's sack
Taking up the seat at the window,
I am swallowing these colors,
They write too many words
For my soul to digest.

Inside the rainbow of courage,
Scrawled in a fog by the little boy
On his grandma's lap,
I see generations of thick skin
Built like the metal
Of this subway track,

We're all moving somewhere,
Collecting sentences in peeling leather seats,
Pages of cubicles,
Learning new shades of skin,

My brain,
This train,
Is due for another stop,
The pen ran out of ink.

- Lea Lumiere

Stones

Each morning
My doubts and self loathing
Place a new stone upon me
Weighing me down
Till my lungs give way
Crushing me, body and soul

- Ruby Jackson

Plaid, Red Flannel

Your plaid red flannel
haunts me as it lingers
in my closet,
touching all my innocent blouses,
my sleepy summer dresses,
my guileless slacks.
You had slipped it to me
one chilly fall eve
when the cold nipped at my shoulders
-an act of a gentleman-
just before it became the only fabric
I wore for you
the night your breath
first skimmed my neck
and you told me
I smelled like rain
and oh
how you held me
like old book pages
and traced the milk of my skin
like the veins of delicate lace.
But now what am I to do?
You're gone,
but your flannel remains.
Each opening of my closet
kindles the coldness I feel in your absence
and rekindles the warmth
and comfort you benevolently gifted me.

You
and your shirt betrayed me.
Because
the plaid red flannel stayed.

- Mel McKinley

Forever an Angel

I still remember that moment, as if it was yesterday. I remember looking into your eyes and seeing for the first time magic in them. You told me to sit down and relax because what you were about to tell me would change my life. Those words, "I'm pregnant," came to me in the slowest motion. I remember calling all my family and friends, telling them of the wonderful news. God! How happy we were then. Every single day, I saw that beautiful glow in your face. I knew that you would be the best mother a child could have. I looked forward to that moment when I would become a father for the first time. In my mind, I was already picturing me holding hands with this beautiful child, me just being a father that I never had. It was that day, when we went to the clinic and they gave us the bad news. I remember holding you tight and my shoulder being filled with your tears. Although I was hurting so much, I couldn't let you see that side of me. I had to be the strong one in that moment. I knew that you needed me more in that time. I told you how sorry I am for it and that it was ok with me, as long as I had you by my side. But see, deep down inside, there was so much pain that I couldn't ever tell a soul. I still

remember getting those emails from a
website, telling me your child is two months
old and so on. It took me six years to dig up
this painful memory that I buried in me. All it
took was looking into the eyes of a beautiful
child and realizing how much hurt I still have
inside.

I know you're in a better place, my child.
Everything happens for a reason. You were
handpicked to be in the arms of the almighty.

- Carlos Medina

Silent Treatment

When I come at you with suffocating silence
and words of written vengeance,
it will be with such patience,
you'll think I've given you a life sentence.

- Cedrik Wallace

Rain Rain

all i remember
from the night you walked away
is the sting of the bullet holes
your truth
left in my heart
the burn of the rain
that soaked my skin
the tears that flooded my lungs
and how i once
never thought
i could be drowned by the rain

- Brittany Bowden

PS

P.S.
I love you as much as my dreams do.

I love you for writing meaning,
into my heart.
I love you so deeply,
that your dimples speak
to me in balanced waves
of two lines that
connect your smile,
then expand in multiple
lines to define every
dust made of star,
and moon on you,
in the sky.

I feel the warmth of your hands
on me, when I lay in a field of
sunflowers that all gaze upon
my now radiant face,
and blue bells that drop
over to caress my skin,
as you do when your
brown eyes analyze
every inch of what you
manifested me to be.

You are an extraterrestrial voyage

from the north to west coast,
diverse landscapes.
Caribbean tropical coast line,
that now encompass the
Amazon jungle.

The quintessence of living energy
in the art of mother nature's assessment.
My reply to recollect every key to your
remedy to unlock every component.

The astronomical elements
of the you, and I align ideally,
as the silhouette of my figure
crosses your intensely, vibrant light;
the awe of our eclipse.

P.S.
I love you as much as my dreams do.
Your sweet, fresh voice that whispers to
my ears on chords that your heart assembles.
The echo, of your lips brushing against mine.

The permanent imprint of your soul.

- Dana.Dane

Fabricated

do you remember
that shirt of mine
that was your favorite -
the grey long-sleeved one
with the black stripes?
i wore it today
and didn't think about you once.

(there's a lie in there somewhere)

- w.b. night

Travels

> "My spirit travels with the wind,
> and it is there we will find each other
> in the dark."

This world isn't black and white, but so many people perceive it that way. I've seen beyond the gray and into a place where even shadows have some light to dance with. I've seen the rainbows after the storms and felt their pain, as if for once they'd like to be granted a wish.

I've felt the wind and how whispers carry. I've heard the trees reaching just a little higher to catch some of those words. Even though this world is often dark and no other souls are in sight, I can still feel you there, like you're right behind me. And if I turn around, I might catch a glimpse of you there. But the space where I feel you is empty.

It's always empty. But if I look beyond what my eyes can see, I will see you in between life and dreams. And if we're both lost, all we need to do is find the wind. She always knows how to bring us home. And it is there we will find each other in the dark.

- Sarah Doughty

Talk Me Down

Talk me down
Silence the sound
of the crowd of critics
and the crying clown
Take my hand and walk me around

The Imposter is in town
He speaks in my ear
tells me too much
and the pure fear keeps me bound
Help me make sure
that my feet touch the ground

When the lie gets too high
Please...talk me down

- Dominic Chianese Jr.

Untitled

the blonde hair was a façade
just a veil of what you thought
they wanted to see
I believe when you stopped
fighting your dark roots
dyed it black instead
and got the tattoos you always wanted
you started to look like yourself
feeling authentic
with a new light in your eyes

- Leigh Greenthorn

Vicious Cycle

I'm shaking, shivering, trembling
even though I'm wearing a hoodie,
my thickest, fluffiest socks
and two comforters.

Is it because I'm cold?
Is it from all the negative, intense
emotions that come along
with fighting suicidal ideation?
Or is it because there are no more liquids or
solids left in my body?

I guess I should be grateful
that my body decided to wait until
my mind had calmed down a little,
to wait its turn to try and pulverize me too.

Mind breaks body breaks mind breaks body
breaks mind and on, and on, and on.
A vicious cycle that is nearly
impossible to break.

Almost
but not entirely
impossible.

I've done it before
which is how I know I will survive this.

It might take me some time
but I'll do it again.

- Ayesha Noor

Cold Veins

As I exhale, mist condensates
prudently on the mirror.
I hesitantly write down what
my mind won't comprehend,
'Love.'

Gradually the mist evaporates, and the words
I cautiously wrote down vanish.
I inhale deeply with the hope
of breathing in new life to melt
the ice crevice around my heart.
Deeply embedded in my thoughts,
there was no reason to seek change.
My mind confined to a box of self-pleasure.
Reclusively unapologetic as I knew no better.
Like a crab, crawling in and out
of my shell as the rain constantly
overshadowed the rainbows.

Insensitive?
Maybe somewhat.
Blame it on the unfulfilled promises that led
to the cold shackles around my mind,
which imprisoned my body and
held my heart hostage.

Until one day,
a ray of light beams on my face

and your radiance illuminates my body.
Your warmth has melted the ice block within,
igniting the diminished fire within me.
Transmitting hope into my veins
and awakening new life just like
the subtle moment
the butterfly emerges from its cocoon.

I exhale,
and the mist is no more.

- Ehinaaya

Adolescence

Carefully, I place myself within the
innocence of my adolescence.
I wander deep within the dreams that
have long since departed me.
My ears intently tune themselves to hear the
soft spoken sounds of my parents.
I await the warmth of the embrace,
as I long to be sung to sleep again.

I am free to roam everywhere
on this island on mine.
Insulated by the happiness of memories.
The ones not tainted by nature's ticking time.
How a mother's love keeps
the dark days at bay.
My soul often roams about in desperation for
a release, for the voice of a once upon a time.

I called for you, as I turned and clambered as
fast as this pre pubescent body would allow.
But it was not quick enough, for when I
reached your location it was access denied,
father gone.
You left me amongst the
litter of human puppies.
Yelping for a parent to feed them, but like
them I was left to drink from the swampy

waters of a broken home.
Brothers and sisters not yet grown,
finding a togetherness in the alone.
Withdrawing into the shadows of adulthood,
of a home, of myself, just me. On my own.

Yet I still wander amongst my dreams,
in the hope of someday I find your
sunlight amongst the shadows.
Awakened dreams as I run out the
school gates joyously into your arms.
Just to be read a story once more, as you
speak of tales as I drift back to sleep.
As I push my own litter on the swings.
I only wish to be the one screaming
higher daddy, higher.

- Jonathan Young

Days Like This

There's no fear in the dark.
It's quieter, and sometimes,
even a little brighter.
Where you can't see what's coming,
or about to hit you.
Like a shot to the heart,
or a thousand lightning strikes.
But there are days like this,
that draw us out past the pain,
to stand in the rain.

- Ragan Rodgers

Shelter

We build a shelter
Out of sticks
Against a fallen trunk
And we call it
Safe.
Someday,
We shall rise beneath
Our rough rafters
And realize -
We've built this life
Around, a decaying spine.
But for now we rest
Content. Believing
In the permanence
Of our edged progress.

- Ashleigh Romano

Goodbye

I'm sad to go
I'm relieved
I'm tired

So much of what makes you, you
Is what makes me, me
The twisted amalgam of feelings and memories
That remain of our messy formative years

Why then, is it so hard for you to understand?
It's been years
To lose hope would be to think you hopeless
And I'm not yet ready to do that

But why does 'gay' still fly from
Your lips as an insult?
Why is queer culture an amusing oddity, to be
Dissected, flirted with, and mocked?
Why do you speak of them as if
You do not know them?

You know me

'But I don't mean you
You're not like that'
Oh I am, brother of mine
I am like them
And I am like you
Do not fracture me for your convenience

Don't you realize
You only fracture the version you get to see
I can't trust you anymore
Not with the things that make me feel the most
You don't deserve them

You get part of me
Part happy
Part relaxed
Part guarded, uncomfortable and ashamed
Of you
Of your displays of arrogant ignorance
Of your fragile ego that thinks it needs them

I like you
I love you
I loathe the part of you that needs
To make others small

Goodbye
I'm going home to glue all
The parts of me back together
The ones you love intermingled
With the ones you hate
That's how they belong

- Ali Finch

In Search of US

My mind, lost to the universe
sought to find you in every
galaxy I came across
But, maybe I was looking for you
in all the wrong places,
those bright shining stars
Maybe I needed to look for you
in those black holes,
I was scared to cross over into
Maybe, your light has dimmed
Maybe, you just needed to be
reminded of hope
So I'll chase the sun
And delve into the darkness
Bringing the light with me
To illuminate your smile once more
When I do find you,
In whichever zone you're hiding in.

- Soshinie A. Singh

Yellow

We started with yellow,
But soon you decided you'll be blue,
And I wanted to be white
So that I could feel your blues.
When you'll be red,
I'd like to be red,
To taste a bit of your anger or hate.
Both ways the driving power is love.
When you'll be grey,
I'd like to be black,
So that I help you take control.
When you'll be black,
We'll finally be together,
Because then you'll be completely mine.
But I wish you to become yellow again,
So you don't feel the darkness I live in,
breath in, every day, every moment.

- Tanisha Khurana

Sin

You see when you raped me,
You didn't just rape my body
You took more than just
Flesh and Blood and Innocence
But a piece of my soul came with you
And I'd like to believe I've healed.

It doesn't pain me anymore
Because I left *it* with you
And somehow, it feels like
You're still a part of me
Like the piece you took
Was also one you replaced
The Flesh, the Blood, replaced
But the Innocence -- that's Sin now.

And I told myself I healed, I swore I did
But I cried again today, sitting in traffic
Thinking about the wounds that had since
Become numb.

Selective memory's not healing,
Forgetting isn't feeling.
I cried for only thirty seconds
Before the blackness returned
And my eyes glazed over
But I wiped those tears,
Cause' when my eyes turn to marbles

They reflect too much fear.

I couldn't say *me too*
I couldn't let my voice feel the words.
I couldn't find the sounds and the consonants
Because even after seven years,
Nothing I ever feel is constant

For nearly a decade, I blamed myself:
I filled every fiber of my being
With crimson, glitter,
Black leather and Blood.

Now I'm older, and for the first time,
Realizing
That's what I was —
A child living in a hopeless world,
Fifteen yet I drank too much.
Fifteen but only liquor tasted sweet to me.
Fifteen and what they told me was
God's greatest gift,
You stole from me.

Although it's been seven years and they
Say that every cell in my body has changed.
They all still scream the same unknown name
Even after seven years,
I still feel the same pain.
No matter how many times *I've forgotten*
The only thing that could steal the breath

Of your sins from my shoulder
Is the breath of *his* love filling my lungs.

And now the Sin you bled into me
No longer ruins me.

- Rachel Chace

Take Me Back

Take me back to yesterday,
When the skies were clear and blue
And the sunshine felt so warm.
When I believed in my religion and
Someone up above watching over me.

Take me back to yesterday,
When love and romance felt so true,
And not like an unclassified religion
I have come to despise. When the
Sound of a beating heart synchronized
To mine brought a smile to my face.

Take me back to yesterday,
When I foolishly believed in fairytales
And forever afters. Before heartbreak
Turned me into a heartless romantic
pessimist waiting for a tomorrow
that may never come.

- KM Quinn

Here Before

I was here before,
when I was ten years old,
but it was with my grandfather.
We were in a hospital room
just like this,
but I didn't know
that it was the last time
I would see him.
He told me that he loved me,
but I never replied;
and it left a hole in me.
I think that's why
I say too much now,
I want to be sure
that everyone around me
knows how I feel for them.

I was here before,
now with you.
They say you have
12-24 hours to live,
and this is the last time
I will see you.
I love you
and even though
you can't say it back,
I know that
you love me too.

- Natalie Jensen

Arsonist

I looked at you
through you
saw your heart
beating fast
a quickened pulse
set a fire
a twin flame
we could not escape
till we burned it down
one inferno
at a time

were we just
arsonists?
living to create love
or were we just cold?

- C. Churchill

Breathe

Breathe.
This is not a poem
This is your Bible for the next few minutes
This is the manual to get you out alive
It doesn't matter who you are
Or what you've been through
If you're reading this, it probably means you
need a hand getting up
And don't we all?
No, I won't ask you to "snap out of it"
Nor will I tell you to "shake it off"
What I will ask of you though, is to inhale
Like it was your only source of oxygen
You tell them you're fine but are you, really?
You're vulnerable and your scars are showing
And it's okay to not be okay sometimes
But it's also okay to put your shields down
and let people in, one at a time.
Smell the hint of petrichor in the air
after a drenching rain
Feel the water caress down your skin
The cold sensation washing
all your troubles away
Do you feel that?
The blood coursing through your veins
Your heart beating strong like the
victorious sound of drumbeats,

Your lips stretching and spreading like a
damn wildfire devouring the universe
Feel it, because that means you're still alive
That means it's not over yet
If you decide to end it today
You may never know what tomorrow holds
You'll never paint another vast blue sky
Never sing another rainbow song
You'll never see another sunrise
at the end of the dawn
And I know this stings and hurts like a bitch
But don't let go just yet
Hold on another moment
Just a minute, just a day
And I promise you,
the Sun will burn brighter for you
And you will soar amidst the vast blue skies.

- Aparajita Bhattacharjee

Don't Look For Me

don't look for me
don't call for me.
please don't.

i wish to remain lost.
somewhere, anywhere,
in the in-between.

this wayward journey
has me forgetting
my way back home.

i have no destination
or the will to be found.
leave me.

these feet will never
turn back towards
you.

- Rose Jay

Grandfather

Though I hardly knew my grandfather
I see so much of him in you.
The ways he found the forest floors
Almost constantly under his feet.
The tone of voice he took with you,
As he spoke softly through a cloud of
whiskey, smoke, and a fear of getting old;
Of getting weak.
The smell of motor oil and spruce that stuck
to your clothing like sap
Every time he held you close
To pass the rough-cut words that only a
father and son can know.
I see so much of him in you,
As you keep me at a distance that stretches
Deeper, and further than the roots of the
Ancient giants in your father's forest.

- Hayden MacKinnon

Remember Me

Find her, sitting here, alone
Oh so damn alone
Questions barreling
Down her throat
Causing her fragile frame
To tense, relentlessly
Coaxing rhymes
To pretend once more
Fuck, the pretending
Always pretending
Playing a part
She auditioned for
But grew tired from
The minute her so called
Number one fan
Threw hateful words her way
Happy, put together, and strong
Is what she wants you all to believe
When in truth, she is
Unhappy, broken, and weak
Mask after mask
One crumbles as another appears
She begins to lose grip on reality
I beg of you to please
Look deep into her eyes
For it's the gateway to her
Tired soul
Dimming with self doubt

Shadows and their deceitful echoes
Greedily take over
Questioning everything
In truth or false
When in the end,
All that really matters
All she needs to know is:
Is she even worth
Remembering?

- Rosa Newport

Rock Bottom

Trying to swim away from the depths
will always be difficult.
Especially when the light reveals how close
you are to the meniscus.
Submerged and swimming with all your
strength, trying to break the surface.

And your greatest fear is being dragged to the
bottom while the surface is so close.
Procrastinating because the insecurities of
failure will weigh you down like
heavy wet clothes.

Stop, strip naked, keep holding your breath...
and sink.
On your way down, allow yourself
to feel everything and don't think.

You will have reached rock bottom now,
tell yourself, I am here.
In the depths of your darkness,
plant your feet on those rocks you fear.

Bend your knees,
raise your chin,
push with all your might,
and feel the water rush over your eyes.

It's your time to rise.

Release your old breath, that for so long
you held dear.
You'll break the surface with such force,
you'll be floating in the air.

And you will remember, you were once at
Rock Bottom

- Mikhail Wolf

The Graveyard

Once in the dead of night
He walked toward her grave
Head hung down in shame
Eyes red and watery
Asking for forgiveness
Apologetic and embarrassed
Took all the blame
Of all the broken promises
And the river of tears she had cried
Her innocence was the first to fall
But it wasn't the end of vicious crime
Now he stood
Explaining the meaning of
Pain agony and strife
But I dismay your final apology
You'll never be forgiven
Even though you repent for the dead
"Make it before you bury
I am resentful"
The graveyard said

- Nikita Nasa

Phases

It's not only the moon that goes through phases - from showing everyone the fullness of its beauty to not showing any of itself - it's people, too. And friendships. And love.

- Joseph E. Cano

Puzzles

Imagine that you're a puzzle.
The first few times you get broken up,
it's easy to put you together
it makes sense
the picture is still beautiful.
Then imagine that you stop breaking
where you're already broken.
Imagine that the pieces start breaking in
halves
quarters
sixteenths
and you lose some of the pieces
and there's water damage
and it doesn't even look like the picture
anymore
and so everyone gets up
and leaves the table
because they don't know how
to put it back together.

That's depression.

- Chloe Frayne

On Letting Go

How do you let go?
When all you desire is to be pulled in closer.
To feel the warmth of the fire you dreamt of
for what seems like lifetimes,
wrap itself around you.
Bringing the rosy color to your cheeks as you
snuggle into the comfort of a blanket
you had been missing.
How do you let go of a feeling that flutters
from deep beneath the darkness, splintering
the ivory, allowing your heart to beat in a
pattern you thought you'd never hear again?
And how do you let go without allowing
the shadow of agony make a home?
When you've finally found that smile, tell me
how are you supposed to let that go?
How do you let go of what makes
you feel whole?

- Cass Marie

Sunglasses of a Hypocrite

A blind man wears sunglasses,
a deaf man can't wear earphones.

A white man had slaves,
a black man chiseled stones.

A silver ring with a golden luster,
a seed of grain in ragged clothes.

A Napoleon with his mighty empire,
a Dylan with his thoughtful quotes.

A general marches for your defeat,
a teacher for your growth.

Shall we say there are no differences,
or differences shall we not note?

Shall we idolize many gods,
or just the creator of the soul?

Shall we be like the glorious rainbow,
or the rain with the righteous goal?

A blind man can wear earphones;
a deaf man, sunglasses.

- Sai Pawar

Running in Place

The truth is,
I'm scared.
I'm scared my time
Is running out
And that I won't reach
The light at the end
Of my tunnel with
My potential fulfilled
That I'll keep
Racing toward
A pipe dream,
While only
Running in place.
I fear growing old
And time won't stop
Years pass quickly
As age adds up.
Tell me it's not too late
That time is still my friend
That dreams should be chased
And that I shouldn't give in.

- JL Smith

Belonging

I don't belong
anywhere.
I never have
and I'm old enough now
to know
I never will.
On my strongest days
I'm able to wear that
not belonging
like a badge of honor,
but in those moments
that I can't outrun
I'd give anything
to fit in
anywhere.

- Jeff Welch

Back

I guess
I just thought,
one of these days,
one of these lines,
one of these poems,
one of these times,
I could finally
write my way
back to you.

- Tiffany Aurora

Initium Novum

We think we'll never breathe again
and our hearts will never beat again,
without the pain,
without the anger raging like a wild fire
through our veins,
without the lump stuck in our
throats and the memories
haunting us like ghosts,
in the middle of the night,
when we've lost all hope,
in the broad daylight,
when the day is too long and the
sun is too bright
and we sit in our cars and we cry,
they ask us if we're okay
and we lie.

We are not okay. We are not okay.

But tomorrow comes anyway,
and the sun will shine through
the darkest days,
and the ghosts won't stay,
and sleep finally comes and hope resurfaces
in the form of a simple smile,
and that fire inside,
it never dies,
but it builds and burns and

it keeps us alive,
and the anger fades out,
and our hearts come back to life,
we remember how to forgive,
we remember how to live,
without the sadness hanging over us like a
rain cloud following wherever we go,
and we learn how to be happy again,
we find things to believe in,
it's never the end,
only a new beginning.

- J. Rose

Bullies

I've let you live inside of me for so long now.
I've listened to all your talks and I let you
hate me. But that darkness has drained me of
everything that I am. And now, now I've
scraped up the only strength I have left to
throw you out. This bully doesn't have a
home in me anymore.

- Nicole Hartley

Georgie

Sometimes I think about those
cool July nights, when the humidity
would break and we'd walk around
the city for hours on end;

wandering the streets littered
with the noise of strangers, always finding
adventure, often looking for dangers.

I think back to that one night when a
June bug got caught in my hair and
we both hated June bugs so we both
just freaked out until you eventually
swatted it out of my hair.

It's strange because I don't even notice
June bugs anymore, since the times
we used to spend together.

- Kristin Kory

Casualty

You were a solider
With a trick up your sleeve
Fighting for a union
Whose values you did not believe

Monogamy was the sword
You could not yield
Ironic that reclusion was your armor
Deflection was your shield
You told yourself
That you wanted this war
As much as I did
But that white flag
Would prove otherwise

Ain't no bravery in retreat
Not after there was so much at stake
I pushed my soul to the limits
Asking it to form the strength
To absorb more than it could take

But you couldn't handle the chaos
You love better in the quiet

So I shed my tears in silence

Picking up my pride
I had tossed aside for you

Turning my back
To the turmoil we created

Saving what's left of me
For the next fight

- Joshua Arion

Living Loss

Loss doesn't always look like a still body in a pine box. Or an urn full of ash; flakes of someone that once was.

Loss can be missing those who are no longer a quick walk away. But they are all still living and breathing. It can be leaving a job or a relationship ending or moving on. It can be change, for better or worse. It isn't always the unfathomable, tragic event of death.

Loss can be living too.

- Julie-Anne Marie

Hugo

Hugo has a cheeky smile and loves to play
metal core on his acoustic guitar. He's
always playing heavy shit and hailing Satan.
But he also has rare, tender moments where
he will sing you Modern Baseball in his
basketball shorts and will look at you as
though he wants to give you the moon. What
he doesn't know is that I took his ex-
girlfriend on two dates and dreamt about her
for awhile. I don't feel bad about it. She was
a goddess in a golden city of four million. I
was a peasant who had nothing to offer but a
drink and my dick. And I didn't even give
her my dick.

- C.C. Lancaster

Knick Knack

I have never stopped drawing
the reflection of myself
I saw in the mirror as a young boy
white, milky skin
large headstone teeth,
a few glimmering with sunlight
capped in silver
bowl cut brown hair
falling evenly across my brow
a fresh heart, learning to beat well
runs down
that glimmer, that starlight
in the brown of my skies
I cannot replicate
time has dulled it
taken the sharp edges away
turning me into a useless blade
the fragments left after years
of erosion, time erodes,
time speaks only in swears
I only write with now
erosion is the only
language that I know
and I have mastered carving
knick knacks out of both
the stones thrown at me
and the ones I am gifted
I place them on my mantelpiece

shine them up real well
and when the sun hits them
early in the morning
we both yawn, and I see
a wet beard, fresh out the shower
skin kissed by the sun
and the reflection of a glimmer
not my own
and I toss the crudely
shaped knick knack
in the junk drawer

- William Bortz

Fire

Let it burn the very darkness
that holds you backs and let
this love be everything about
growth and prosperity. But if
the fire burns out, the love
loses its meaning and turns
into a routine of chores that
the body completes for the
sake of it.

Bring down such lifeless
leafs from the branch of
life and let new life take
place as you are meant
to live for the fire that
makes you want to burn
your soul for a brighter
tomorrow.

- Parth

Storm Chaser

there is thunder
in this heart of mine
but i always did prefer
the company of those
who ran toward the rain
despite knowing
that natural disasters
do not fit comfortably
in palms
despite knowing
that storm-chasers
most often return
empty-handed
with little to show
less wind-whipped cheeks
and the elusive
taste of wild
that lingers
on their lips

- Kelly Luna

Pain

There are different types of pain.
But no matter the form, all agony
announces it presence.
It demands an audience.
I know Pain.
We have been well acquainted for years.
Lifetimes even.
Bones break and there it is to remind you of
the mistake, to form tears in your eyes every
time you move the wrong way or the rain
comes to play years down the road.
Hearts shatter.
Literally and figuratively as you fall in love
and fall apart,
Despair is there to sober
your thoughts of hope.
Years of never being enough, but always
tough on the outside and brittle within,
too close to breaking.
Too close to the skin that was grabbed too
harshly and judged guilty of being too
imperfect to love but too perfect not to take.
And it will Hurt.
It will hurt when you are lost and the memory
of the time you thought you were found is
also the memory of when you were
left on the ground.

And it will sting when you're lonely but not
so alone and your mind keeps playing
telephone with your heart and not a single
one remembers the correct message,
so you wander in the shade as it becomes the
darkness and you bade farewell to the
moment when Pain, was simply a paper cut
on your pinky finger.
I know Pain.
I know it well.
And it makes me feel so damn alive.

- Melissa Marie

When Awareness Meets Bravery

Have enough confidence to
recognize you are a sunset.
Enough humility to remember
the sun and earth that made you.
And enough bravery to
return to yourself,
over and over again,
no matter how many times
the night takes you.

- Erin Van Vuren

Misguided

I no longer look for you among the stars. I gave up the notion that you could still be watching me. Guiding me through right and wrong. I chose my own path. One that you did not approve. I read different stories now. Ones of love and loss and romance and heartbreak. I threw away the book that you told me to cling to. One that told stories of pain and hatred. I no longer live to please. I live to experience and grow. You told me if I was good I would be rewarded. You took everyone I love away from me. When I asked you what I had done to deserve this you turned away, no explanation granted. I can hear their pain. The ones you ignore. They plead with you to save them from the world you created. You just left us to destroy each other until finally, you no longer claim us as your own.

- Amy Littleford

Sorry

I sit dead on my couch
Like someone put a bullet into my head
The tele flashes light
On the darkness that fills me
The stench of the smoke
Fills my motel room and pretty much my life
Don't know how we ended up here
Waiting for the skies to part
And throw us a miracle
Baby how I wish I could tell you that
I am dying to run back to you
Dying to kiss you one last time
Dying to say that I love you
But I'm sorry
I had to break your heart
This is the love but it's impossible
In this life time or maybe more

We've got to wear a mask
And live this lie
You there and me here
Worlds apart, lifetimes apart
Pretend we are absolutely dry
When the truth is
That this rain soaked us really deep
Lonely as I am
Baby, I have to let you down
And hold back my bleeding heart

And say this to you
I am dying here
To run back to you
Dying to kiss you one last time
Dying to say that I love you
But I'm sorry
I had to break your heart
This is the love but it's impossible
In this life time and yes maybe more

Life can't break me anymore
Than I already am
Pieces of me lie
On this dusty rug in this
Godforsaken motel room
This whiskey on IV
Slowly numbs this stabbing pain in my heart
But it still hurts
And it is still there,
You... are still there
Nothing helps
The drugs, the alcohol
Believe me I have tried
Nothing dulls it
It's carved in stone
I'm sorry it had to be this way
But let me call you
One last time
And tell you that
I am dying to run back to you

Dying to kiss you one last time
Dying to say that I love you
But I'm sorry
I am so sorry
I had to break your heart
The only heart that I possibly want
And a love that is so fucking impossible
In this lifetime and definitely more.

- Sakshi Narula

No More

No more staying quiet
I refuse to do so
No more keeping my mouth shut
over a man taking
something that is not his
No more staying quiet over
a child whose meal is a wish
No more accepting a single bloodshed
by a man's fist
No more hiding behind full cover makeup,
or blaming it on nonexistent clumsiness
No more allowing a child to hide
under his bed when he hears his mother
begging for her husband to stop
To stop hurting her, not because
she's afraid for her life
But because she's afraid her child
might hear her cry
Our bodies
Our decisions
"Your body"
"Your decision"

- Saide Harb-Ranero

Focus

I'll focus on me
and the rest
will either
fall into place or
out of the way.

- Amie

Penguin Poetry NYC

Letter to Bryan – Anna Lete

Dear Bryan,

Yesterday, you told me you were god.

Gods are ignored.

You will scream from your throne, calling
your children by the names you gave them,
until your voice turns to blood, and you are
forced to walk the earth you created to show
yourself again to those you left behind. You
will go into houses of worship made for you
and no one will recognize who you are. You
will perform miracles in a desperate attempt
to lure them back to you. But they called you
doctor. They called you teacher. They called
you science. They called you mom, dad.
They called you Google.

Gods are forgotten.

You had your fifteen minutes of fame.
Time's up! Move on. Too bad you didn't
cash in on it while you could. Too bad
everything was just recorded in a book
passed down from one generation to another.
So sit back. Relax. And watch another show.
Watch another great invention. Watch

another new discovery that originated from you. Watch another display of power. Watch another idea become reality and hear their praises that don't give thanks to you. Keep watching.

Gods only exist if you believe in them.

You better start counting. Count your disciples. Count your followers. Count your people. Count the broken souls you thought would stand by you because you healed them. Count their prayers. Count their tears. Count their wounds. Count their words. Count. Where are they now? Where are your disciples? Where are your followers? Where are your people? Where are the broken you healed?

I don't want to be god.
I am the wind.

You feel but do not see. That gives and takes. That blows wherever it wants you to go. That whispers. That calls. That howls and demands to be heard. That needs a response. That you cannot control.

I am the fire.

You cannot put out. That ravishes and destroys everything it comes into contact with. That stands in its path. That doesn't give way. That finds a home in darkness. That sets hearts ablaze with want and longing and dreams. That provides. That warmth. That gives. That hope.

I am the sea.

You cannot walk on. You will be taken by my waves. You will be dragged by my current. That you cannot breathe under. That you cannot be saved from. That you will drown in. That will teach you to overcome me.

I am the ground.

You abuse with each step you take. That is overused by greed. That is overrun by innovation. That I allow. I allow all of it. Because I also am the void that you seek and fall into when you cannot find peace.

Yesterday, you told me you were god.

Today, I tell you, I hold your world together.

Love, Anna

High School Sweetheart - Casandra Rojas

Truth is, I miss my best friend.

Remember when back in 7th grade,
you said you hated me? I should have
believed you then. You ignored me on every
occasion, but I found you again in 10th
grade. There we were. I stared hard as every
bit of the way you moved seemed to
disregard me. I should have heeded the
warning. Instead, I showed up and charmed
you with serpent like gestures. But I was far
from venomous. You on the other hand had
the grin of a class-A predator. I wish I could
have seen past the gleams, a pretty smile, and
a chuckle in my direction and I was blinded
by the bright attention; I should have caught
the distractions. But I was busy while it
happened. Far too preoccupied with keeping
you hypnotized. In your tongue was the knife
and when it met mine by the end of the night,
all was dark except for the fire now inside.
You left and I should have come to then,
instead, I called you. Hours holding a phone
cord like trying to keep that high note in
choir practice. The Girl Scout crew said I
seem distracted. I only allow me to hear my
thoughts wandering off.

Yellow

How many more times until you stay?

11th grade, not a day goes by that we don't do everything together, including argue. You pushed me that one day. I fell ass-backwards on the sidewalk. Fuck. You cried, remember? Then, apologized. I realized that day. But still ignored myself, even forgave the clear honesty in your eyes. Not when your crocodile tears dropped, no, but when you put your hands full force on my shoulders and shoved. Shoved my love and concern down the sewage drains of Main Street, about 7 blocks away from the courthouse, and 4 blocks from where we had tied this knot. Connecting your vengeful abuse of power with my relentless fortified need to give love. I should have heard the cracking beneath me, should have listened to mother Earth when she shouted on impact. My helpless body just sat, then got up and hugged your back that was turned toward me. The county library was the next time we would coincide for such a scene. It's an absolute mystery how I still miss those streets just as I miss the kid I grew with, next to, learned so much from.

You lived with me at this point. We were almost seventeen and we shared a royal red comforter with golden decorations all over it. Although when sleep came, we used each other to cover all the frostbitten parts of our bodies. My house burned down that winter and by summer, you were gone again. When I began working for your mother, I swore to myself there was no way possible I would fall for you ever again. This time my witty intelligent brain was determined. No way, not ever. The hatred in your honey-dipped cinnamon-laced eyes was enough to completely shut me down. You tried to run into my car with your leg; I sped off, somehow though, thirty minutes later, I was pouring potions over the lesion on your knee and we were back in a roller-skating rink, wobbly slippery floor beneath us and those god damned circles.

High school sweetheart. I graduated, you were elsewhere. When I left, I did not say a word. And Twelve years later, I miss my best friend.

Shadows - Danneile Davis

As a child, I was scared of the dark.

I met each night with dread, tucked as deep in my bed as the comforter would allow, vainly requesting a nightlight as though I actually intended to sleep there by myself. The light was small, but warm: just enough to allay my fears, just enough so I could fall asleep.

Until the nightmares would come for me anyway and my parents would wake to find me a hair's breadth from falling off their bed, snoozing peacefully.

The nightmares never stopped. But my patience with the fear did, so I decided one night to confront the dark.

I closed the door. No light from the hallway. I left off the nightlight.

Pitch black.

My chest tightened, and I hurried blindly to my bed to draw the comforter. But then, the strangest sensation came over me…

Serenity. I felt calmer and more at peace that night than I ever had.

Which is when I realized: I wasn't scared of the dark. I never had been. And I certainly wasn't scared of the light.

I was scared of the shadows.

Scared of the distorted figures looming over the walls, lurking furtively in the corners of my room. Scared of the warped interplay of not-quite light against not-quite darkness, drawing monsters and mayhem across my anxious mind.

Scared of the unknown. Scared of the in-between. Scared of the uncertainty.

Shadows can take so many forms. They're the murky seawater harboring sharks or seaweed; the morning fog-obscured shapes belonging to children or mailboxes—but time has shown me others. They're the legalese of a housing lease, the smile of a business adversary.

They're the way you talk to me.

They're the warm tenderness of your gaze, and the draftiness of an impersonal text. They're your thoughtful attention to detail, and your twice-repeated: "commitment-phobia." They're the sincerity of your concern, and the elusiveness of your vulnerability. They're the endearments slipping like honey from your lips, and the other words still seemingly stuck in your mouth.

Shadows.

I've only seen two solutions to shadows: the bright light or the pitch black. Childhood made my decision simple, but time compounds fear until it suffuses everything in grey.

Now I'm scared to turn on the light. In raising questions that warrant answers, in robbing the shadows of their strength, I may inadvertently reveal truths I'd hate to see. About you? About me? That murky water has a chance of harboring just seaweed, as long as you don't reveal the sharks. But still, wouldn't it be better to know? Than to let them keep smothering every word I want to say?

And darkness? To snuff this thing with darkness, shut off all hope, and close the door on us? Therein lies a solution I suppose, but hardly the answer. There's no comfort in this kind of darkness. Besides, I was scared of spiders as a child too—but killing a spider never killed the fear. In fact, I'm still scared of spiders.

And as an adult, as your lover… or maybe something more…

I'm still scared of the shadows.

Blank Pages – Paula Lopez

Blank Pages
Blank pages with lines that need to be filed.
Blank pages I wish I could incinerate.
Waiting on the very last second
for your return.
Nothing. Nada. Zilch.
Silence is all I hear.
No laughter.
No cry, not even a goodbye.
Silence louder than our fights.
Blank pages.
Why can't I just leave them blank.
Six months. Manila folder.
Judge signature, it's done.
Fairy tale gone wrong.
Fake promises.
Fake dreams.
Fake late night loving.
All the memories you forgot to keep.
Patiently I waited,
accompanied by whiskey and lime.
I thought I would be happy to
see my maiden name in ink.
I open the flap out of that pretty manila
envelope. Hoping for the loudest hooray!
<pause>
I crumble to the ground.
My face to my knees yelling your name

to the silent walls.
Louder than I've ever cried
your haunting name.
My mascara left marks on the carpet
eternalized the reality that my marriage
was done.
Thirteen years. Just like that.
Erased from time.
No more best friend.
No more kisses to my head.
No more Sunday brunch.
No more dancing to our song.
No more makeup sex.
No more I Love You.
No more forgive me please,
I'll never do it again.
<pause>
I cried for loss.
I cried for change.
I'm finally free, I said.
So, why do I feel a prisoner to your absence?
To your name?
I will always miss you.
I will always love you.
I will always pray that you never
hurt the way I do.
As I hold these papers you refuse to see.
I will carry the pain for the both of us.
I will love our children for the both of us.
I will thrive.

Yellow

I'll get up and rise
from these ashes you left behind.
I will hold on till the last second
of my dying breath.
Hoping.
Hoping.
Hoping
For your return.
So we can burn these blank pages
to the ground.

2920 Days - Captain Grawlix

I wrote you a note
when we were 19
that said
I value my pen
above all things, save for one,
a girl whose brown hair
that crackles in the sun
until I swear it's red
not like your mom's
but like a little furnace,
the one in our first apartment
where we sat in front of
eating pizza
and talking about how when
we turned for help
there was that massive void,
a vacuum of people
willing to love us,
and you were the only one
who understood that,
because every time
I screamed into the void,
I did it alone
except in March
and in April
when I spent
my first year with you–

fuck,
I love you,

--and I wrote that this pen
was in service of that one
wonderful being,
and that's
an emphasis on
wonder,
like how we saw a baseball game together
and you sat two rows ahead
and looked back at me and smiled,
I thought the moment would
only live in my head
but someone,
I forget who,
snapped a photo,
and I saw it
and died
and came back to life again
in the same instant

fuck,
I love you so much
I can't finish my thought

My pen, is in service to you

And when I shut the door
behind me

saying
I need to write this down
it became heavier and heavier,
the pen,
I mean,
to pick it up
while you go to bed alone
and I keep saying
THIS IS FOR US
THIS IS FOR US
when I know,
laying with you
until you fell asleep
would be for us
kissing your forehead as you close your eyes
would be for us
drawing your eyelashes
holding your hand
reading to you
would have been for
us.

--
Eight years
and it took me three
to say I love you
and seven
to say it every day.

I want to see year one me

and shake me and say
why are you the way you are.
Love isn't this angry.
Love doesn't tally good deeds.
Be kind
you fool
be kind.

I want to see year two me
and remind me of that Cure song
when I sat alone in my apartment
smelling of French fries
and how
when it came on
I wrote a little note
that said
call her
and I would add
marry her.

I want to see year three me
and say
it's okay to be vulnerable
to tell her you're afraid
you're not a person she can ever love
and how you don't believe her
when she says she loves you
because you don't believe anyone
has ever really loved you.
God damn it, say

something
you fool

I want to see year four me
and tell myself
let her heal you
she is the only one
who can put you back together
and that
it won't be the last time
you need to cry in her arms
and let her comb your hair
and let her stay awake,
she wants to stay awake
and for once,
watch you fall asleep

I want to see year five me,
hey,
year five was amazing.
You know it.
And never forget that
she brought you lunch,
and that her booty looks
excellent in those shirts
that are kind of like dresses too.

I want to see year six me
and say
anger is not a substitute for love.

Yellow

You fucked up,
and saying
"I'm this angry
because I feel so much for you"
will never
ever
ever
justify trying to hurt her
on purpose.

And if I could take back
year seven I would
for it was the first time
I ever chose these flimsy words
over you.

But eight, asleep,
is infinite,
and forever I want to
dream with you.

--

This poem is for you.
I love you.
I love you.
I love you.
I love you.
I love you.
I love you.

100

God,
there isn't enough times
I can repeat it to fill in the spaces
when I didn't say it
or I refused to say it
or I said it and didn't feel it
hold on
I love you
I love you
I love you
that's it,
there's nothing more.
Because love has no beginning,
only our part in it does.
I love you
without beginning and without end.

Paciencia - Tomislav Kurtovic

Paciencia
Lo que yo digo es
Paciencia Sabali, Patience –
That's the first thing overheard
at the airport --

Día-a-Día. Poco-a-Poco.
Little by little, day by day,
Puerto Rico se levanta.

My baby can only drink a special kind of
formula, she's colicky. So any others will
irritate her. That's her in the picture, on the
top. Here, too, look, this is what our home
looked like before the storm, before this
mess, it was beautiful. It's still beautiful.

I've lived here my whole life and I'll die
here.
Here, in this home that we built.
Here, where we raised our kids.
Here, overlooking the ocean, with most of
our things laying in a pile of rubble and half
our doors, hanging half off the hinges.

This is who I am --
Esta casa Esta tierra, Puerto Rico.
(yo no me quito)

My husband was the one who parked the car
on the other side of the river. After Irma, he
knew this was gonna be a real one. He's also
the one who put in the generator -- It's
industrial grade.

They had to bring it in with a crane. They
parked it down there on the main road, and
dropped the generator down like this, from
the street below:

I know everyone who lives on that street.
Every single person; you believe it?
Everyone who lives on this side of the river.

Don't believe me?
If you take the road further up away from the
collapsed bridge, you'll meet Milagro, who
lives with her family in a little yellow house,
with three guard dogs. Pass her place and
you'll get to Fernando and Anna, then Maria,
Angel, Jesus, Juan, Anna, and Eva,

But then there's this one guy, whose name I
always forget, I can never think of his name.
So I call him the dandy.

He's always dressed fly whenever I see him.
He's got a straw hat, white shirt, clean pants,

shiny shoes, nice watch, everything, looking good, always. So I call him the dandy. I can never remember his name.

But that's OK. I know him and he knows I know him.

This is who I am -- Esta calle,
Esta tierra, Puerto Rico.
(yo no me quito)
Día-a-día, Poco-a-Poco,
Little by little, day by day,
Puerto Rico, se levanta.

My brother took the upstairs room with no roof and all the puddles of water, where the mosquitoes bite. They don't even bite, they chew. Those things are this big, but he stays up there, getting rained on every day, so we can have his room on the first floor and so the baby is not getting bit all day, all night.

It's tight, but we make it work. It's been good except when last time it rained and the river flooded up to our waist, up to here. It's been tough to smile, but sometimes a smile is the only thing that keeps me going. A smile from my husband when he finally comes home, to this tight little room, after 12-hour days from dawn to dusk.

A smile from me,
A smile from my baby,
A smile from my daughter,
A smile from my brother.
Sometimes a smile
Is the only thing
That keeps me going.

(yo no me quito)

Día-a-Día Poco-a-Poco,
Little by little, day by day
Puerto Rico se levanta.

My father needs me here. He's getting up
there in years and he doesn't have a lot of
help. I had to take a month off of work so I
could help him rebuild. I'm glad my job
understood -- It's hard to find help here
because everyone's so busy dealing with
everything that they're going through.

People got no roofs, no things, no home,

So it's not easy to ask for help but we make it
work. People still come. People still make it.
Everyone looks out for each other, we're like
a family.

Yellow

(yo no me quito)

Do you know, at 95, they've never cut me
open once, not once? I've never had them cut
even one of my fingernails. Not even one
fingernail! And the only pills I take, are
sometimes when I have trouble sleeping. So I
take 2 before bed to help me sleep. I have so
much energy! Sometimes I need a little help
getting to bed. I feel happier now than I've
ever been. How could I not feel that way?
After surviving, this monster, what is there
not to be happy about?

I have my home, my neighbors, my family.
My family.
Do you know how many grandkids I have?
Fourteen!
I have seven kids, eight great-grandkids,
GREAT-grandkids!
No wait, eight kids, and seven great-
grandkids!
Yeah, that's it.
I always mix them up.
But it's definitely fourteen grandkids.

How could I not be happy?! Fourteen
grandkids! And I'm grateful for every day,
every breath that God has given me. That

God continues to give me. I've never been
happier!

This is who I am Esta familia
Esta tierra Puerto Rico,
(yo no me quito)
Día-a-día, Poco-a-Poco,
Little by little, day by day
Puerto Rico se levanta

This is who I am
Esta isla
Esta tierra
Puerto Rico.

(yo no me quito)

Still Mine - Terri-Lea Cassidy

I often think I have let go of him,
forgotten even. It is never truly the case
though; the smallest thing can bring him
flooding back in. A song, a word, a person
walking by with the same olive complexion,
a shabby hair do, a voice, an outburst in the
street. He's always there, and yet he hasn't
been for so many years now.

I have blocked so much of our time
together, but I do still remember a lot, things
I wish I could forget. Running in the street.
Riding our bikes. Getting ready for school.
Even all the fights and the teasing, it's all too
painful to remember, because I wish that we
could both be back there.

Nobody in the whole world has a
smile that could match his. It was always
huge, with his two little top fangs gleaming
in its broadness. It was carefree, even though
he never was. He had a small frame, but the
largest shoulders out of anyone I've ever
known.

I remember one time when we were
in the pool, it had a strong filter and we were
having fun trying to swim against it, like an

ocean current. I was so small though, and weak, I could never make it through no matter how many times I tried. He told me to hold onto him, and he was strong enough to pull us both to through to the other side. I would never be strong enough to do the same for him.

We were driving across the Nullarbor once, and he became excited over every eagle we came across, cutting through the silence with childish joy. He had this innocence about him, like nothing could touch him. Now I see that isn't true, everything touched him. He was just a lot better at hiding it than the rest of the world.

I have spent many years placing blame for losing him. I blamed our mother, for the bad choices she made, and for being what I believed was weak and selfish. I have blamed my dad, for not doing enough for a son who wasn't his. I have blamed my mum's second husband, just for being the awful man he was. I have blamed our cousin, for thinking it was okay to touch him the way he did, and my aunt for turning a blind eye. I have blamed a god I don't believe in, and a mental health system that failed him. I have blamed a substance, and I have blamed myself, for not being a better sister. I have also blamed him. I have blamed him for not being strong enough, for not caring enough, and for not turning into the man I know he could have been, the man he was supposed to be.

He loved the Simpson's, Marvin the Martian and The Flintstone's. We would play hide and seek and cricket and video games together. He was really good at Alex the Kid, it was no challenge for him and he clocked the game time and time again. He loved reading the Goosebumps books and I'm pretty sure he owned all of them. He was really good at drawing and had the neatest hand writing you will ever see.

I don't remember when he started changing, I didn't pay much attention, I was too wrapped up in watching everything else falling apart to notice that he was being ripped to pieces. I often ask myself if it was a slow progression or something that happened quickly. The answer doesn't really mean anything anymore though. I wish that none of it mattered.

I looked up to him. He was my big brother, and now he's gone.

"Hello?"

An echo of his voice tumbles down
my spine. Could it really be him? It sounds
like him. Could he really still be in there,
after all these years? I thought he had
escaped through the needle marks that line
the arm of a body he once held, but maybe he
didn't. Maybe he is still in there, begging to
be heard, to be seen, to be remembered.

I go to see him, and I look into his
eyes. Mostly, they are vacant, empty, a void
of black, brown, red and white. But every
now and then, for just a millisecond, there is
a flash, a flash of consciousness trying to
return, a flash of a struggle between child and
beast.

He's nervous. His body twitches, his eyes
dart back and forth faster than I can follow. I
wonder which side of him is nervous. Is it the
child, the beast, or someone in between?
Which part of him is more afraid? Is he afraid
of being lost, or is he afraid of being found?

We sit in silence, across from one
another. It has been years since I have felt his
presence. I think a part of him may actually
be trying to return.

His head goes down, he seems small, and defeated. When he looks back up, his eyes have changed again. They've gone dark. I can't see passed them, they're like a forest of twisting branches and giant webs. I could see him before, trying to fight back, but now he is gone again.

Now he is back to being no one.
The hope comes and goes like dust in the wind. Always passing through, but never finding a safe place to settle.

The Black Capricorn - Harry Huang

"Is this seat taken?"

Angela shakes her head. She stares at him, the strange man wearing black. He's young, nineteen or perhaps twenty, but no older. His hair is thick and messy like a dense forest; it's impossible to see his forehead. When he smiles, he dispels an air of boyish innocence, but this is just an act. Behind those gentle black eyes gleams a jagged cunningness—ingrained in his face like the cut of a perfect diamond.

"May I sit?" he asks.

"Go ahead."

He immediately makes himself at home, setting his belongings on the table: a lighter, a pack of cigs, a golden timepiece. The watch is beautiful; he cannot have paid for it himself.

"Do I know you?" she asks.

"Do I know you," he repeats.

Angela rolls her eyes. What an ass.

"Do you know me? It's curious that you ask this question," he says.

"How come?"

"Because if you did know me, then you wouldn't have bothered. Rather, a better question would be: Who are you?"

"Okay, smart-ass. What's your name?"

"What's your name," he smirks. "Another curious question."

What is up with this guy? To have the audacity to approach a girl at a coffee shop and make her feel uncomfortable, this guy must really think he's something else.

"I don't agree," Angela says. "It's perfectly ordinary to want to know the name of the person you're sitting across from."

"But do you really want to know?"

"Wouldn't you?"

"Not really. Names are terribly uninteresting. They don't tell you anything about a person other than what to call them in bed." He leans forward. "Say, I don't mean to be rude. I know I've come across as pretentious and perhaps arrogant, but that was never my intent. I am a curious person, and sometimes, I phrase my curiosity in unsightly ways. This is a bad habit of mine, one I've been meaning to correct, but haven't had the time. Let's start over. Is that all right?"

"I guess."

He smiles. "Can I assume you asked for my name because you want to understand me better? In that case, why not ask what I'm doing here? Or what I like to do with my free time? Or perhaps, how many cigarettes I smoke a day? I assure you, any one of these questions will tell you more about me."

"Okay," she says. "How many cigarettes do you smoke a day?"

"Interesting."

"What?"

"Interesting that you chose that question. In a sense, I had phrased my choices in the present: What I am doing here. The past: What I like to do with my time. And the future: How many cigarettes I smoke a day."

"I don't see the connection between your smoking habit and the future."

"You are asking me when I'm going to die."

Angela leans back, pauses, and blinks several times. "You're drawing a lot from thin air."

"Am I?"

"Yes."

"Well then. Can I assume you're not a smoker?"

"How can you tell?"

"A smoker can always tell," he says. "Your hands are perfectly still. Not hungry. Smoker's hands are always craving for something—not necessarily a smoke, just something. A lot of people smoke because they have busy hands. It has nothing to do with addiction."

"Is that what you tell yourself?"

"Yes."

He adjusts his seat so it's closer to her; she pushes hers back to even the distance to what it was before.

"Okay," he says. "So ask me the question again, more directly this time."

"What question?"

"Your question about the smoking."

Where is he leading her with this? Part of her doesn't want to know, but the rest is fascinated.

"Go on," he says. "I promise, it won't hurt to ask."

Fine. "How is smoking connected to the future?"

"Not that question. The other one."

"Which question?"

"Ask when I'm going to die."

"Why would I do that?" It seems like a very personal question to ask.

"To amuse yourself. We all need to be amused, or else what's the point in living?"

Angela frowns. "When are you going to die?"

"In fifteen minutes."

The young man reaches for his carton of cigarettes and leans back into his chair. He shakes the carton up and down, removes a smoke and sticks it at the corner of his mouth. Then, he pulls his lighter from the table, flicks the switch several times, but only manages to create a feeble ember. He shakes his head, sighs, and focuses on Angela. "Say, any chance you have a lighter?"

"You already know I don't smoke."

"Aha! You got me there." He grins.

She doesn't grin back. "Is it true?"

"Is what true?"

"Are you really going to die?"

"Do you care? Will my life or death impact you in any way?"

"Of course."

"What if we'd never met, if someone else had been sitting here instead, and you'd found my obituary in the newspaper? Would you still care?"

"No. I'd skip to the horoscopes."

"I like you," the young man says. "For a girl who doesn't smile, you have an excellent sense of humor."

"So do you."

"Oh? Why thank you, but what for? I haven't been joking." His unlit cigarette twirls between his fingers like a glow-stick. "I'm really dying." He reaches toward the table, and picks up his golden timepiece. "See this watch? It's a special device. It's designed to tell a person the exact minute and second they're going to die. Who needs a crystal ball when you've got one of these?"

Angela glances at the watch. "It says twelve minutes."

"Then it's going to happen in twelve minutes," he says. "See? Better than magic."

"Why would you wear something like that?" Angela says.

"Why not? At least I know how much time I have left, and can spend it wisely. Like a wallet, I find it easier to keep track of cash than credit."

"But the timer doesn't bother you at all? I'd be freaking out."

The young man shrugs, as if to say no big deal.

"Does this mean I'm the last person you're ever going to talk to?" she says.

"Yep. Big pressure, right?"

"Yeah, I mean." Angela raises her palms, and they turn up empty. "What do I even say? I feel like every word I tell you has to be meaningful. But I'm not a fortune cookie. Maybe you should talk to someone else."

"Don't fret," the young man says. "My death will be of little consequence. I'm not the president, or a saint, or anything like that. You can start talking about a Big Mac and fries, and it'd be perfectly suitable for my last conversation."

"Oh. In that case, I really like Scarlet Johansson's new hairdo."

"Really? I'm dying and you want to talk about a miscellaneous celebrity's new hairstyle?"

"You said you didn't care."

"I was wrong. Now I realize my mistake. Sorry, but this dying business is not as funny as I thought. Death is serious. I mean, people don't decorate their headstones with quotes by Scarlet Johansson."

"Oh. Well, I don't know what to say." Angela taps her forehead, as though knocking for an answer. She muses over famous last words she's heard in movies. For some reason, Martin Luther King comes to mind. The Beatles too, even though Paul McCartney is still alive. Perhaps she could tell the young man about his horoscope.

"What's your sign?" she asks.

"Capricorn."

She raises a newspaper that had been discarded on the table, folds to the back and finds his horoscope. "It says: A big change is coming today, but you'll need a stranger's help to make it happen. Don't be afraid to

119

talk to them. It's easier than you think." She sets the newspaper down. "Wow. That really nailed it, don't you think?"

The young man nods. "It was pretty good. But I can't shake the idea that the advice would apply to anyone, no matter what their situation was."

"You're such a buzz kill."

He scans his watch, and then turns to Angela. "Well, here's the good news. I only have six minutes. Then you'll never have to deal with me again."

Angela doesn't respond.

Neither does the young man. He flips his unlit cigarette between his two pointing fingers back and forth. The cigarette dances like a gymnast flipping through monkey bars. It makes a baton swirl, then it stutters against his nails, and falls to the table. He frowns, and looks up at Angela. "What if I told you that you could save my life?"

"Oh." Of course. Angela draws a deep breath. She should have known better. "I don't have any money. If that's what you want, you should've picked a better target."

The young man waves his hand, as if swatting the notion away. "I assure you, I'm not making a play for your money. If that were the case, the gentleman behind you would be a far more suitable candidate. I'm only proposing a hypothetical question. If you had the chance to save me, would you?"

"Of course," she says.

"Didn't you hesitate a moment ago? What if it cost you money? Would you still do it?"

"Depends how much."

"So the truth emerges. My life has a price." The young man smiles. "Okay. Now it's your turn to amuse me. Please. Tell me how much you'd be willing to spend to save my life?"

"Let me think." Angela begins to chew the nail on her index finger, a habit that she can't seem to get rid of.

"Can I ask you a question?"

"I was trying to think," she says.

"I'm sorry, go on."

Angela scans the young man up and down, lets her imagination run wild, and then says, "Two thousand dollars."

"Okay, now may I ask my question?"

"Go ahead."

"What factored into my price tag? Does it matter what clothes I wear? The value of my belongings? Did I get an extra grand for having a charming smile? Or did you take a grand off because I talk too much?"

"All of the above," she says. "The smile cost you a hundred though."

"Ahh." The young man flashes his teeth. "I got these from my mother. I suppose, I should thank her for making my life a better bargain." He closes his mouth, and then opens it again as if caught in the middle of a yawn. "Say, how much would you pay for your own life?"

"Everything."

"That was fast." The young man falls back, staggered. "I'd almost have thought you were answering your own question. It's curious though." He taps the table, several times. "There's no limit to how much you'd pay for yourself. Is that correct?"

"Yep," Angela says.

"Yet most people wouldn't outright declare they are worth more than the person next to them. At least, not if they are humble."

"There's nothing wrong with being honest."

"True." The young man begins to glow. "The human mind is fascinating."

"Not really." Angela shakes her head. "It's just human nature. We're wired to survive, but not to help others survive."

"Strange. Is that how you can sit across from a dying man, and have a casual conversation? You haven't once offered to help me."

"Excuse—"

"I'm sorry. I wasn't trying to point out any fault with your behavior. You're far more normal than I am. I'm simply fascinated by my current situation. You have no idea how much fun it is to die." The young man says, then rises, shuffles his belongings together, and distributes them equally among his pockets.

"You're leaving?" she asks.

"Yes. I've got four minutes left. If I don't leave now—Well, you don't want to know what happens."

Angela opens her mouth to speak, but only manages a murmur.

"Come again?"

"It's nothing."

"Are you sure?" The young man skims his watch briefly, and then looks back at Angela. "This is your last chance. I've asked you so many questions. It's only fair that you have the same chance to ask me one."

She bites her lip and nods. "How's it going to happen?"

"Ah. I see. Well, it's—"

"Never mind," Angela says. "I don't want to know. I've changed my mind."

"Are you sure?"

"Yeah."

The young man scratches his chin. "You really don't care? What if I'm dying because of food poisoning? Don't you want to know where I bought my chicken sandwich?"

"It'll be on the news. If not, then it'll already be too late for me."

"Suit yourself." The young man leaves a five-dollar bill on the table and heads toward the exit. The waitress doesn't wave goodbye. Angela wonders if she would have bothered if she knew his situation. Then, a thought occurs to Angela. She slaps a ten-dollar bill on the table, gets up, and leaves the café.

She enters the sidewalk. Cars of all assorted colors buzz in front of her like a blurring rainbow. She turns her head left and right and catches a glimpse of the young man several yards ahead of her. One hand is tucked in his pocket; the other holds out his timepiece. She skims her own watch and performs a quick calculation. Based on what the young man said, he has two minutes before he dies. She continues after him.

The closer she gets the faster he walks, as if her proximity pushes him away.

Why is he hurrying? She wonders. Where is he going?

He reaches the end of a street, where the crosswalk sign flashes.

DO NOT WALK. The young man, unconcerned, continues through the traffic aimlessly like a blind man taking a stroll. And yet, as if fate itself has a vested interest in the outcome, he reaches the other side, unmarked.

Angela's approaches the same street corner. Cars whiz ahead of her at forty miles an hour. DO NOT WALK flashes with thirty-five seconds beneath it. She scans the traffic light, the cars, and then her watch.

She steps one foot onto the road.

BEEEEEEEP.

She yelps back.

DO NOT WALK counts down to twenty-eight seconds.

She looks at her watch. The young man has less than a minute to live.

She looks back at the street. It is no more inviting now than it was seven seconds ago.

She steps her foot forward one more time.

BEEEEEEP.

She grits her teeth. She looks back and then forward. She puts her head down and charges.

BEEEEEEP.

She sees the young man in black. He's not far. She calls to him. He doesn't hear, so she screams louder. The young man pauses as though tapped on the shoulder. "Come back," she says. "Come back." He turns around. She continues through traffic. "Come back!" She crosses the double yellow lines. "Come back," she cries. "I've got the money." The young man faces her, standing sideways like a shadow, black eyes pulsing like an eclipse: Black… Cold… Piercing… One finger points to his watch, another finger at Angela. He stares deep into her eyes. They throb. Thump. Thump. Thump. Angela freezes, compelled by a riddle: What's your sign? My sign? Signal. Traffic signal. Stoplight. Stop. She screams, "Stop—

Acknowledgments

Where do I start when there's a community of people I want to acknowledge? The most important people are my Penguin team. Carlos Medina, KM Quinn, Jennifer Rose, Saide Harb-Ranero, and Casandra Rojas. They are definitely the of heart of the team and have truly taught me what family is.

A few people that were there during moments that Penguin Poetry needed them most: Wade Staark, Kris Duncan, Myke Duarte Carlos, and Melissa Marie. You will always hold a special place in our family. Thank you for your love and support. It has not gone unnoticed.

I couldn't have put this book together without every single writer in here. I'm proud to include all of them in this collection.

I am so grateful to Sarah Doughty for the beautiful dedication and foreword. Sarah also created our incredible cover and she is a constant support to not only us but everyone in the writing community. Thank you for always being there to offer advice, hear us vent, and answer questions!

I wouldn't have been able to make this anthology as smooth without Soshinie A. Singh. Thank you so much for catching all of the mistakes I missed and for creating the Kindle version of this collection! Soshie is someone who has been a friend to everyone on the Penguin team. She is a force of good and kindness in this community.

I have so many other people I wish I could include. I hope you all know how much you are appreciated by the Penguin Poetry family. We will always be your safe space. Please remember that.

Yours truly,
Nicole Hartley

Author	Title	Pg
Ali Finch	Goodbye	34
Amie	Focus	80
Amy Littleford	Misguided	75
Anna Lete	Letter to Bryan	82
Appy Bhattacharjee	Breathe	44
Ashleigh Romano	Shelter	33
Ayesha Noor	Vicious Cycle	26
Britt H	Illusion of Love	6
Brittany Bowden	Rain Rain	19
C. Churchill	Arsonist	43
Captain Grawlix	2920 Days	95
Carlos Medina	Forever an Angel	16
Cas Rojas	High School Sweethearts	85
Cass Marie	On Letting Go	55
CC Lancaster	Hugo	67
Cedrik Wallace	Silent Treatment	18
Chloe Frayne	Puzzles	54
Dana Dane	PS	20
Danneile Davis	Shadows	88
Debjyoti Ghosh	The Storm	4
Dominic Chianese	Talk Me Down	24
Ehinaaya	Cold Veins	28
Erin Suurkoivu	Mon Adieu	10
Erin Van Vuren	When Awareness Meets Bravery	74
Harry Huang	The Black Capricorn	113
Hayden MacKinnon	Grandfather	47
J. Rose	Initium Novum	60
Jeff Welch	Belonging	58
JL Smith	Running in Place	57
Jonathan Young	Adolescence	30
Joseph E. Cano	Phases	53

Author	Title	Pg
Joshua Arion	Casualty	64
Julie-Anne Marie	Living Loss	66
Kelly Luna	Storm Chaser	71
KM Quinn	Take Me Back	41
Kris Duncan	Song of Eve	2
Kristin Kory	Georgie	63
Lea Lumiere	Subway Scars	12
Leigh Greenthorn	Untitled	25
Mel McKinley	Plaid Red Flannel	14
Melissa Marie	Pain	72
Mikhail Wolf	Rock Bottom	50
Myke Duarte Carlos	Addict	8
Natalie Jensen	Here Before	42
Nicole Hartley	Bullies	62
Nikita Nasa	The Graveyard	52
Parth	Fire	70
Paula Lopez	Blank Pages	92
Rachel Chace	Sin	38
Ragan Rodgers	Days Like This	32
Rosa Newport	Remember Me	48
Rose Jay	Don't Look For Me	46
Ruby Jackson	Stones	13
Sai Pawar	Sunglasses of a Hypocrite	56
Saide Harb-Ranero	No More	79
Sakshi Narula	Sorry	76
Sarah Doughty	Travels	23
Soshinie A. Singh	In Search of Us	36
Swati Barik	Permission	9
Tanisha Khurana	Yellow	37
Terri-Lea Cassidy	Still Mine	108
Tiffany Aurora	Back	59
Tomislav Kurtovic	Paciencia	102

Author	Title	Pg
W.B. Night	Fabricated	22
Wade Staark	Gifted Regret	5
William Bortz	Knick Knack	68